# CHRISTMAS JOKE BOOK

Published by Collins
An imprint of HarperCollins Publishers
Westerhill Road
Bishopbriggs
Glasgow G64 2QT
www.harpercollins.co.uk

HarperCollins Publishers
Macken House, 39/40 Mayor Street Upper, Dublin 1, D01 C9W8, Ireland

In association with National Geographic Partners, LLC



First published 2024



ISBN 978-0-00-869413-5

10 9 8 7 6 5 4 3 2 1



A catalogue record for this book is available from the British Library.

Printed in India.

This book contains FSC™ certified paper and other controlled sources to ensure responsible forest management.
For more information visit: www.harpercollins.co.uk/green

If you would like to comment on any aspect of this book, please contact us at the address on the left or online.

natgeokidsbooks.co.uk
collins.reference@harpercollins.co.uk

Publisher: Michelle I'Anson
Head of Creative Services: Craig Balfour
Text: Richard Happer
Layout: Jouve India, based on a design by Craig Balfour
Editorial: Samuel Fitzgerald
Cover design: James Hunter
Production: Katharine Willard

NATIONAL
GEOGRAPHIC
KiDS
CHRISTMAS
JOKE
BOOK
Ha Ha
Ha
300
LAUGH OUT
LOUD JOKES

1

KNOCK KNOCK. Who's there? CANOE. Canoe who? CANOE HELP ME bake my CHRISTMAS CAKE?

2

Why do DONNER and BLITZEN get to take so many COFFEE BREAKS?

Because they are SANTA'S STAR BUCKS!

3

Did you hear about the CHRISTMAS SNACK that was arrested for SABOTAGE?

It was a MINCE SPY!

**Did you KNOW?**

Henry VIII was the first English king to enjoy turkey, back in the 16th century.

# A BELLY FULL OF LAUGHS

4

**What happened to the GERMAN CHRISTMAS BREAD?**

It was STOLLEN!

5

**What do you DRAIN your CHRISTMAS POTATOES in?**

An advent COLANDER!

6

**How does Good King Wenceslas like his PIZZA?**

DEEP PAN, CRISP and even!

Hee hee!

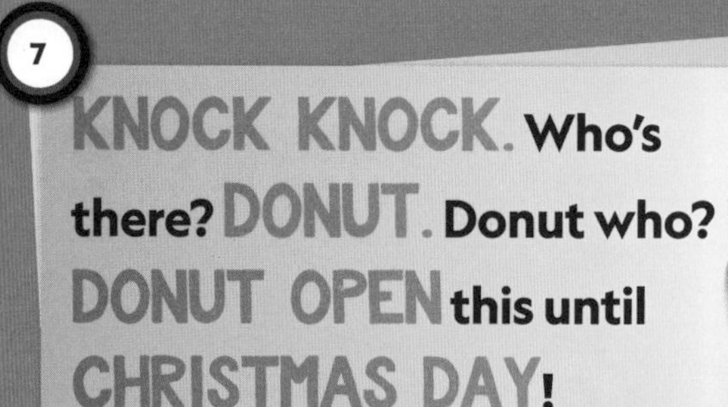

7

**KNOCK KNOCK.** Who's there? **DONUT.** Donut who? **DONUT OPEN** this until **CHRISTMAS DAY**!

8

What did one **CRANBERRY** say to the other at **CHRISTMAS TIME?**

**BERRY CHRISTMAS!**

YUMMY!

9

**Did you hear about the man who drowned in his CHRISTMAS PUDDING?**

He got dragged in by a **STRONG CURRANT!**

# A BELLY FULL OF LAUGHS

10

What did the TEDDY BEAR say when he was asked if he wanted SECONDS?

No thanks, I'M STUFFED!

**Did you KNOW?**

Mince pies are sweet today, but in the Middle Ages they were more savoury and contained minced meat.

11

What did the ROSEMARY say to the sage?

SEASON'S GREETINGS!

12

I'm on the CHRISTMAS TABLE, but you can't eat me. What am I?

THE DISHES!

13

KNOCK KNOCK. Who's there? PIZZA. Pizza who? PIZZA ON EARTH and goodwill toward men!

PIZZAAAA!

14

What do SNOWMEN have for BREAKFAST?

ICE CRISPIES

15

What happened to the TURKEY at Christmas?

It got GOBBLED!

YIKES!

# A BELLY FULL OF LAUGHS

16

**Mum, can I have a DOG for Christmas?**

No, you can have TURKEY LIKE EVERYONE ELSE!

**Did you KNOW?**

The UK eats 25 million Christmas puddings each year!

17

**What's a SNOWMAN'S favourite food?**

CHILI!

18

**How do you feel when you can't get to your ADVENT CALENDAR chocolate?**

FOILED.

19

**Why did the GINGERBREAD MAN go to the doctor?**

He felt CRUMMY!

20

**What do STRAWBERRIES sing at Christmas?**

Tis the season to be JELLY!

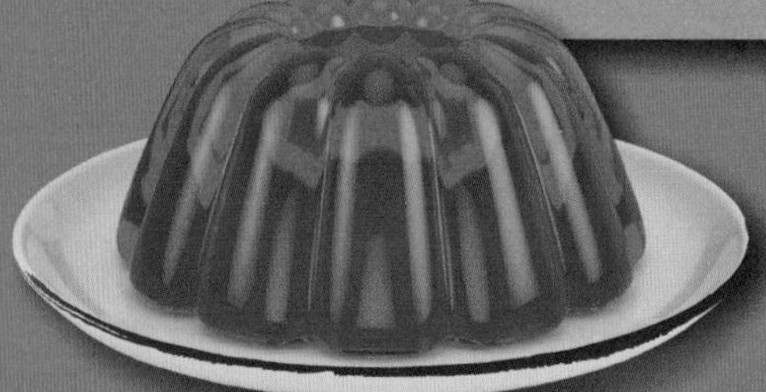

**Did you KNOW?**

The oldest Christmas fruit cake in the world is over 140 years old – yum!

21

**What's a vegan's favourite CHRISTMAS CAROL?**

SOY TO THE WORLD!

# A BELLY FULL OF LAUGHS

2

Waiter, waiter, this TURKEY tastes like an OLD SOFA...

I thought you liked STUFFING!

23

Why doesn't SANTA eat JUNK FOOD?

It's bad for your 'ELF!

24

What's the best thing to put into a CHRISTMAS CAKE?

YOUR TEETH!

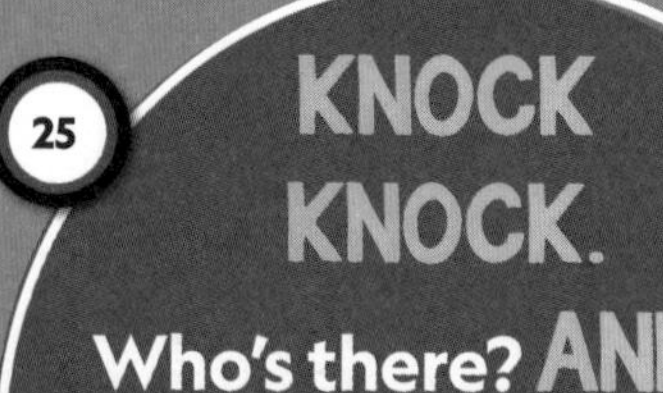

**25** KNOCK KNOCK.
Who's there? ANNA.
Anna who? ANNA PARTRIDGE in a PEAR TREE!

**26** What CAROL is heard in the DESERT?

O CAMEL ye faithful

**28** Why does the TURKEY always play PERCUSSION?

It's got the DRUMSTICKS!

**27** What do VAMPIRES sing on NEW YEAR'S EVE?

AULD FANG SYNE

29

What's a FARMER'S favourite CHRISTMAS SONG?

I'm dreaming of a WHEAT CHRISTMAS!

**Did you KNOW?**

The first song ever played in space was "Jingle Bells" in 1965! Astronauts performed it aboard NASA's Gemini 6A space craft.

30

KNOCK KNOCK. Who's there? WAYNE. Wayne who? WAYNE in a MANGER.

31

**KNOCK KNOCK.** Who's there? **IMA.** Ima who? **IMA DREAMING** of a white Christmas!

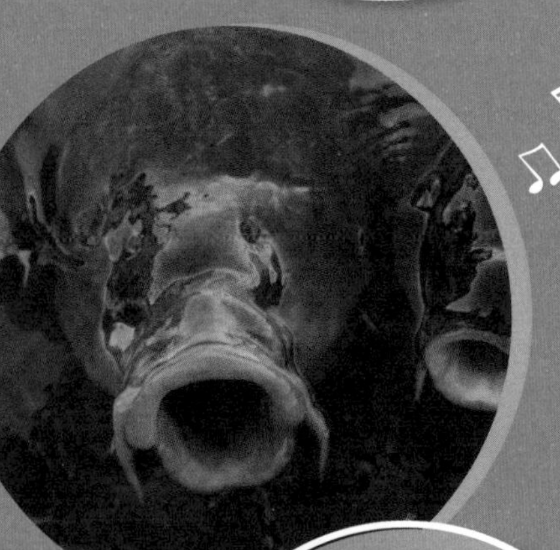

32

What do **fish** sing at **CHRISTMAS TIME?**

**CHRISTMAS CORALS!**

33

How does **TARZAN** know it's **CHRISTMAS?**

He hears **JUNGLE BELLS!**

# PULL THE OTHER ONE, IT'S GOT BELLS ON!

**34** Which Christmas carol was written by a DUCK?

In the beak MIDWINTER

**36** What's a PARENT'S favourite CHRISTMAS CAROL?

SILENT NIGHT

**35** Why did the elf take a nap in the FOREST?

He wanted to sleep like a LOG!

## Did you KNOW?

"White Christmas" by Bing Crosby is the biggest-selling single of all time, with 50 million copies sold.

37

**KNOCK KNOCK.** Who's there?
**WOODEN SHOE.** Wooden shoe who? **WOODEN SHOE LIKE TO KNOW** what you're getting for **CHRISTMAS!**

38

**What do you get if you cross a SHEEP with a TRAMPOLINE?**

A woolly **JUMPER!**

# SCARF-OUT-LOUD FUNNY

39 What did the hat say to the SCARF?

You HANG AROUND here while I go on AHEAD!

40 Why didn't the STOCKING eat Christmas dinner?

He was STUFFED!

## Did you KNOW?

40% of Christmas jumpers are only worn once each year.

41 Why is a FOOT an ideal CHRISTMAS PRESENT?

It makes a good STOCKING FILLER!

42 What ATHLETE is warmest in winter?

A LONG JUMPER!

43

KNOCK KNOCK. Who's there? SANTA. Santa who? SANTA CHRISTMAS CARD to you. Did you get it?

Did you KNOW?

Santa's red costume was made popular by adverts for Coca Cola – before that he was often depicted wearing green!

44

What's RED, WHITE and GREEN all over?

Santa Claus with TRAVEL SICKNESS!

45

What kind of MOTORCYCLE does Santa ride?

A HOLLY DAVIDSON

46

## Where does SANTA keep his MONEY?

In a SNOW BANK!

47

## Where does SANTA stay when he goes on HOLIDAY?

In a HO-HO-HO-TEL!

48

## Why did Santa get a PARKING TICKET?

He left his sleigh in a SNOW PARKING ZONE

Did you KNOW?
As well as organising presents, busy old St Nicholas is also the patron saint of children, sailors, pharmacists - and Aberdeen!

# HO HO HO!

49

**KNOCK KNOCK.** Who's there? **SANDY.** Sandy who? **SANDY CLAUS** is coming to town.

50

Why does **SANTA** always come down the **CHIMNEY?**

Because it **SOOTS** him!

51

How does **SANTA** measure the length of his **SLEIGH?**

In **SANTA-METRES**

52

Why is **SANTA SCARED** of **CHIMNEYS?**

He's got **CLAUSE**-trophobia!

53

How do you **WASH** your hands at **CHRISTMAS?**

With hand **SANTA-TISER!**

54

How much did **SANTA PAY** for his **SLEIGH?**

Oh, nothing, it was **ON THE HOUSE!**

55

**KNOCK KNOCK.**
**Who's there?**
**INTERRUPTING SANTA.** Interrupting Sa- **HO! HO! HO!**

56

**What goes "OH OH OH"?**

Santa walking BACKWARDS

57

**How do you know SANTA is good at KARATE?**

He has a BLACK BELT!

58

**Who's SANTA'S favourite POP STAR?**

BEYON-SLEIGH!

59

**How did SANTA CLAUS open the front door?**

He used a TUR-KEY!

60

**How do you know when SANTA'S AROUND?**

You can sense his PRESENTS!

**Did you KNOW?**

In Germany, children receive presents from Santa on 6 December, which is St Nicholas' Day.

61

KNOCK KNOCK.

Who's there? COLE.

Cole who? COLE SANTA, it's nearly CHRISTMAS!

## Did you KNOW?

Kids in Iceland aren't visited by Santa, but by 13 pranksters called the Yule Lads!

62

What does SANTA'S DOG want for Christmas?

A MOBILE BONE

63

What do you get if you cross Santa with a DETECTIVE?

SANTA CLUES!

# HO HO HO!

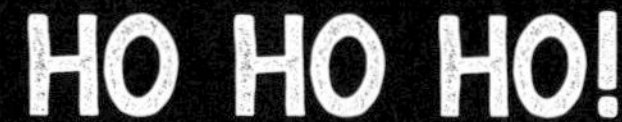

64

## Which one of SANTA'S REINDEER is the fastest?

DASHER

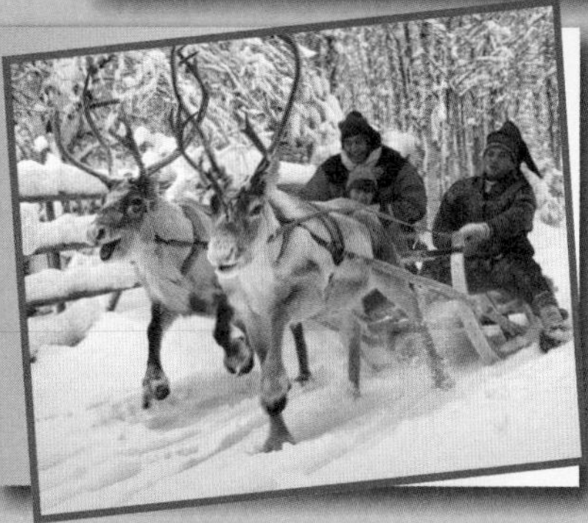

65

## How did Santa get lost on CHRISTMAS EVE?

He was MIS-SLED!

66

## What's the difference between a REINDEER and a KNIGHT?

One slays a dragon, the other DRAGS A SLEIGH!

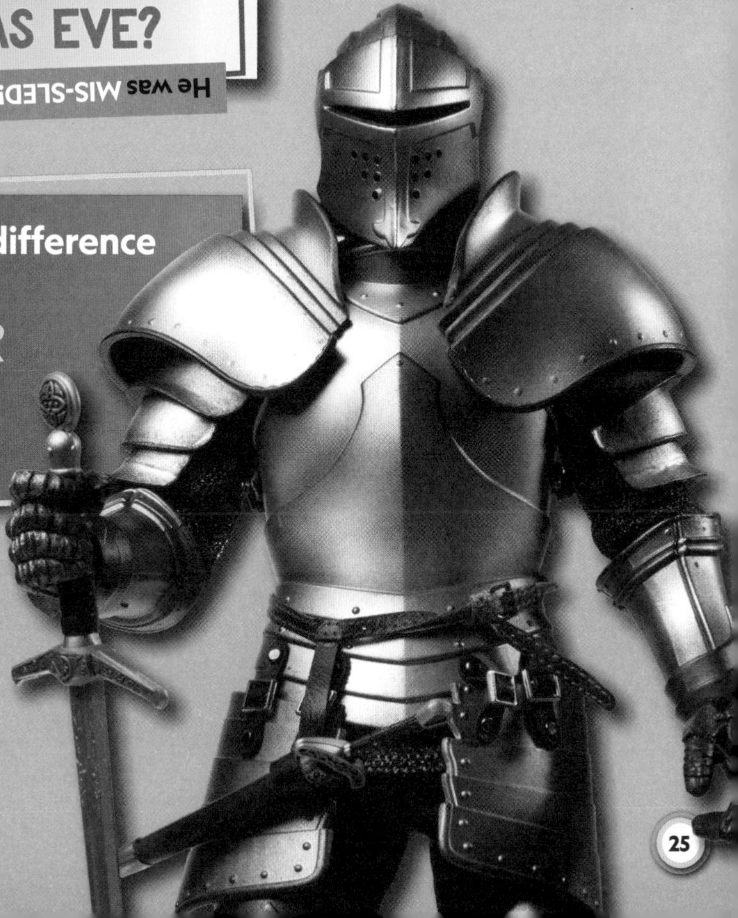

67

**KNOCK KNOCK.** Who's there? **HO HO.** Ho Ho who? **YOUR SANTA IMPRESSION** needs a little work!

## Did you KNOW?

Santa was issued a pilot's licence by the US government in 1927!

68

What goes **HO HO WHOOSH, HO HO WHOOSH?**

Santa going through a REVOLVING DOOR!

69

What is **SANTA'S FAVOURITE PLACE** to deliver presents?

IDAHO-HO-HO!

# HO HO HO!

70

## Who does Santa call when his SLEIGH BREAKS DOWN?

The ABOMINABLE TOWMAN!

71

## Where does SANTA CLAUS GO SWIMMING?

THE NORTH POOL

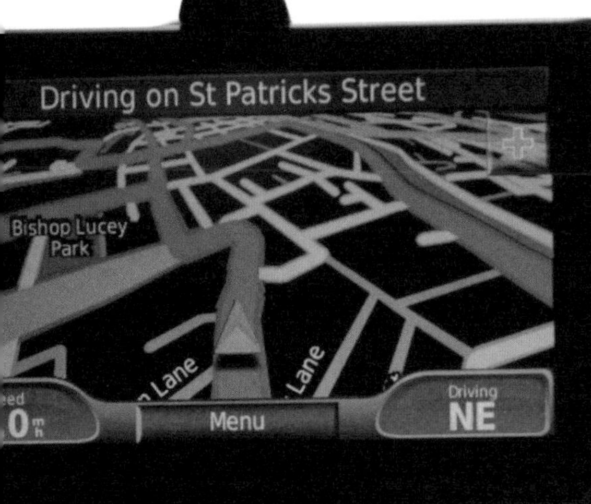



72

## Why does Santa use GPS?

He doesn't want to be a LOST CLAUS!

**73**

## KNOCK KNOCK.

**Who's there? SANTA.**

**Santa who? SANTA CLAUS, DUH!**

**74**

## Where do SANTA'S HELPERS go to work out their problems?

AN ELF-HELP GROUP!

**Did you KNOW?**

Santa's outfit used to be green, not red.

**75**

## Who is SANTA'S FAVOURITE SINGER?

ELF-IS PRESLEY!

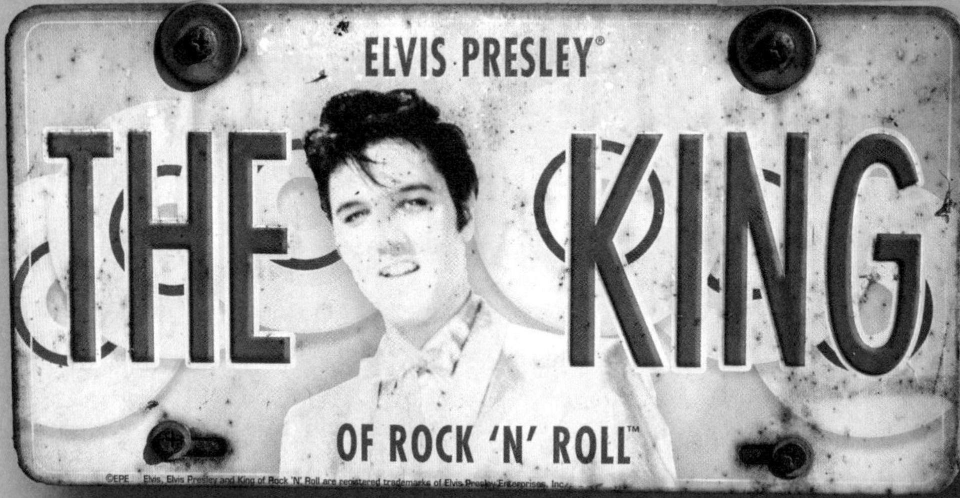

# HO HO HO!

76 **What did the ocean say when SANTA FLEW OVER?**

Nothing. IT JUST WAVE!

77 **What do you call SANTA when he TAKES A BREAK?**

SANTA PAUSE

78 **What NATIONALITY IS SANTA CLAUS?**

NORTH POLISH

**KNOCK KNOCK.**
Who's there?
**ELF.** Elf who?
**ELF ME WRAP** this present for Santa!

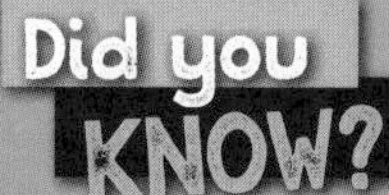


There's no land at the North Pole – just huge ice floes, 2–3 m thick, that float on the surface of the Arctic Ocean.

What do you call a **GREEDY ELF?**

ELFISH!

What kind of **MUSIC** do **SANTA'S ELVES** like best?

WRAP MUSIC!

# ENJOY YOUR ELF

82

If there were **11 ELVES** and another joined them, what would he be?

THE TWELF

83

How do **ELDERLY ELVES** get around?

They use a CANDY CANE!

84

What kind of **PHOTOS DO ELVES TAKE?**

ELFIES!

85

KNOCK KNOCK.
Who's there?
YULE. Yule who?
YULE never know.

86

What do you call an elf wearing EAR MUFFS?

"Anything you like, HE CAN'T HEAR YOU!"

## Did you KNOW?

Under the North Pole's ice, the water is 4,000 m deep.

87

What does an elf do AFTER SCHOOL?

His GNOMEWORK!

Why do SANTA'S HELPERS have to wear HARD HATS?

KNOCK KNOCK.
Who's there?
ELF. Elf who?
ELF I KNOCK again will you LET ME IN?

90

What do ELVES LEARN IN SCHOOL?

The ELF-ABET!

ABCDEFGHI
JKLMNOPQR
STUVWXYZ

91

KNOCK KNOCK.
Who's there?
WALTER. Walter who?
WALTER you ASKING SANTA for Christmas?

92

Who do SANTA'S HELPERS CALL when they're ill?

THE NATIONAL ELF SERVICE!

Hee hee!

## Did you KNOW?

The first explorers reached the North Pole in 1909. The team was led by American Robert Peary.

93

What cars do ELVES DRIVE?

TOY-OTAS!

# ENJOY YOUR ELF

What do you call an OBNOXIOUS REINDEER?

RUDE-OLPH!

Why is everyone so THIRSTY at the NORTH POLE?

There's "NO WELL, NO WELL"!

What do you call a CHICKEN at the NORTH POLE?

LOST

KNOCK KNOCK.
Who's there?
ANITA. Anita who? ANITA start wrapping these CHRISTMAS PRESENTS!

What does SANTA spend his WAGES ON?

JINGLE BILLS

# ENJOY YOUR ELF

99

What did the TEACHER say to her ELVES?

LINE UP IN JINGLE FILE!

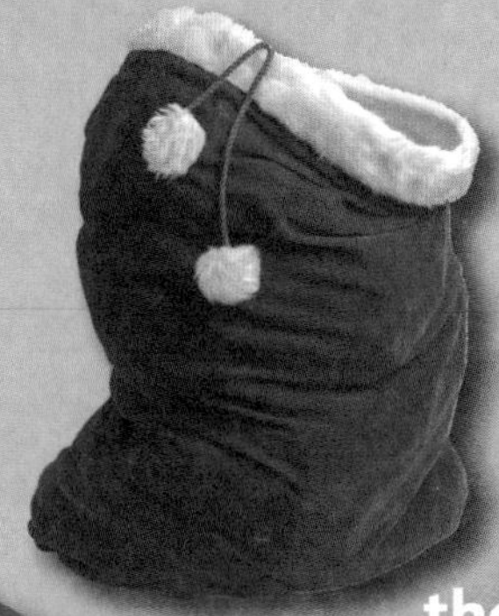

100

What do you call a SNOWMAN that can walk?

SNOW-MOBILE

101

Why aren't the ELVES WORKING ANY MORE?

SANTA GAVE THEM THE SACK!

102

Where do SANTA'S REINDEER stop for COFFEE?

STAR-BUCKS

## Did you KNOW?

The sun rises and sets once each year at the North Pole. It rises at the spring equinox and stays in the sky for a full six months before setting at the autumn equinox for six months.

103

**KNOCK KNOCK.** Who's there?
**SNOW.** Snow who?
**SNOW TIME** for telling Christmas jokes.

104

What do you call an **ELF** that just won the **LOTTERY?**

WELFY

105

What do **ELVES** cook with in the **KITCHEN?**

UTINSELS

# ENJOY YOUR ELF

106

Why was SANTA'S HELPER SO SAD?

BECAUSE HE HAD LOW ELF-ESTEEM!

What's an ELF'S favourite SPORT?

NORTH POLE-VAULTING

108

What do elves use to make LAST-MINUTE repairs?

IG-GLUE!

**Did you KNOW?**

Every year there is a marathon at the North Pole, run by particularly tough athletes!

## Did you KNOW?

Tinsel was invented in Germany in 1610 and was first made from shredded silver!

109 **KNOCK KNOCK.** Who's there? **OH, CHRIS.** Oh, Chris who? **OH CHRISTMAS TREE**, oh christmas tree...



Te hee hee!

# THAT'S A CRACKER!

110 What do you get if you cross a bell with a SKUNK?

JINGLE SMELLS!

111 Did you hear about the BAUBLE who was addicted to CHRISTMAS? He was hooked on trees his whole life!

112 What do you get if you EAT CHRISTMAS DECORATIONS?

TINSELITIS!

113 What's another name for an ARTIFICIAL CHRISTMAS TREE?

FAUX FIR

114

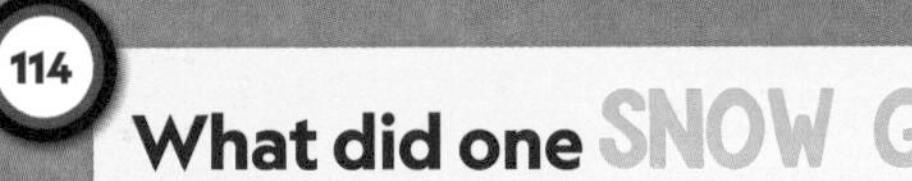

What did one SNOW GLOBE say to the other?

I FEEL A LITTLE SHAKEN!

115

## Why does Santa have three GARDENS?

So he can HOE, HOE, HOE!

116

## What did the Christmas tree say to the ORNAMENT?

"QUIT HANGING AROUND!"

117

## What do RHINOS hang on their Christmas tree?

HORNAMENTS!

### Did you KNOW?

Inventor Erwin Perzy created the first snow globe by pouring semolina into a glass globe filled with water!

# THAT'S A CRACKER!

118 What's the most popular TV SHOW at Christmas?

HOLLY-OAKS!

119 What happens to Christmas trees on VALENTINE'S DAY?

They get all SAPPY!

120 I'm TALL when I'm YOUNG, SHORT when I'm OLD. What am I?

A CANDLE

121

**KNOCK KNOCK.** Who's there? **MARY.** Mary who? **MARY CHRISTMAS!**

122

**What do you get when you cross a Christmas tree with an iPAD?**

A PINE-APPLE

123

What did one **CHRISTMAS TREE** say to the other?

LIGHTEN UP!

## Did you KNOW?

Christmas crackers didn't "crack" when first made in the 1850s. They only had a sweet and a motto inside.

# THAT'S A CRACKER!

124 Why are Christmas trees so bad at SEWING?

They're always dropping their NEEDLES!

125 What did the Christmas tree wear to STAY WARM?

A FIR COAT

126 I come with many colours so BEAUTIFUL and BRIGHT, I turn so many houses into a beautiful sight. What am I?

CHRISTMAS LIGHTS!

127

KNOCK KNOCK. Who's there? ARTHUR. Arthur who? ARTHUR ANY more PRESENTS?

128

Why wouldn't the CAT climb the Christmas tree?

It was afraid of the BARK!

129

What was Santa's FAVOURITE SUBJECT in school?

CHEMIS-TREE

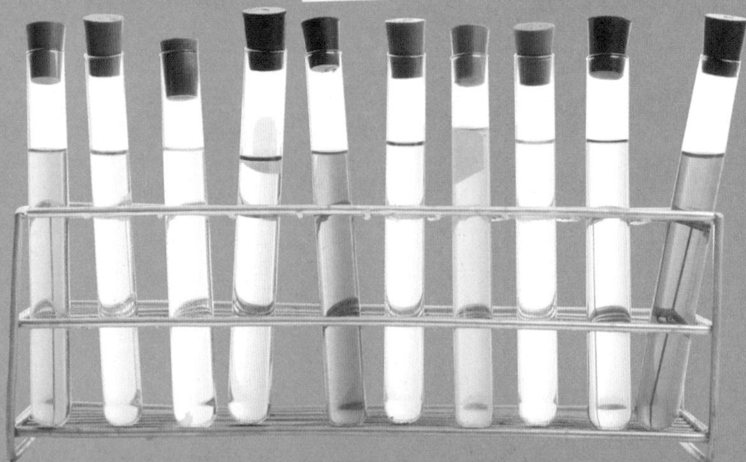

# THAT'S A CRACKER!

0

My friend just won the **TALLEST CHRISTMAS TREE** competition. I thought to myself, "How can you top that?"

1

What's a Christmas tree's favourite **SHAPE?**

A TREE-ANGLE!

2

How did the **TWO RIVAL CHRISTMAS TREES** get along?

They signed A PEACE TREE-TY!

**Did you KNOW?**

The first nativity scene was staged by St Francis of Assisi in 1223 – with live animals!

**KNOCK KNOCK.** Who's there? **KEN.** Ken who?
**KEN YOU HELP** me decorate the Christmas tree?

?

## Did you KNOW?

Hanging up green plants like holly and mistletoe has been a winter tradition since before Christmas was celebrated, originating in ancient Egypt and Rome!

134

What do a **DOG** and a **CHRISTMAS TREE** have in common?

Their BARK!

# THAT'S A CRACKER!

135

**Why did the CHRISTMAS TREE go to the DOCTOR?**

It was looking A LITTLE GREEN!

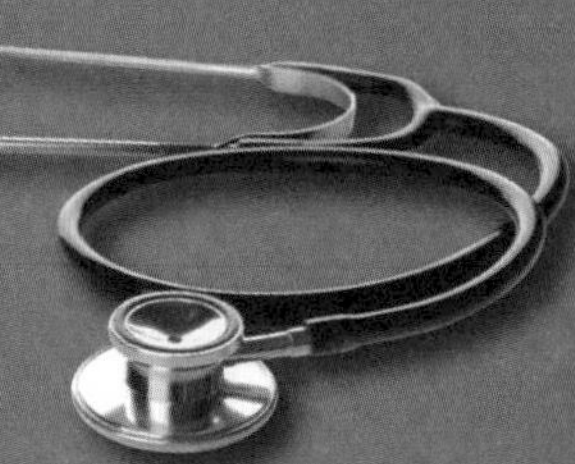

136

**What did Santa say to MRS. CLAUS when he saw their CHRISTMAS TREE?**

It looks okay, but you could SPRUCE IT UP A BIT!

137

**What do you call CUTTING DOWN a Christmas tree?**

CHRISTMAS CHOPPING!

138

**How do CHRISTMAS TREES get their EMAIL?**

They LOG ON!

139

**KNOCK KNOCK.** Who's there? **FIFI.** Fifi who? **FIFI FO FUM** I smell the blood of an Englishman!

140

Why did the **PANTOMIME PONY** have a sore throat?

It was a LITTLE HOARSE!

**Did you KNOW?**

The baddies in pantomimes always enter the stage from the left-hand side!

141

Did you hear that the **WIZARD** in this year's **PANTO** has a **DOG?**

It's a LABRACADABRADOR!

# HE'S BEHIND YOU!

142

I asked the **LIBRARIAN** for a book on **PANTOMIMES**. He said, "**IT'S BEHIND YOU.**"

Why is a **PANTOMIME** often just called a **PANTO**?

Because **MIME IS SILENT**

144

On which side of the house did **JACK'S BEANSTALK** grow?

**THE OUTSIDE**

145

KNOCK KNOCK. Who's there? SARAH. Sarah who? SARAH GIANT living here?

146

Unfortunately CINDERELLA didn't make it as a FOOTBALLER. She kept running away from the ball.

147

Did you hear that SNOW WHITE has taken up a new career as a JUDGE? It makes sense – she is the FAIREST of them all.

# HE'S BEHIND YOU!

148

An actor I know kept falling through the floor in **PANTOMIME**. I think it was just a stage he was going through.

149

Why shouldn't you steal a **GIANT'S HARP?**

Because it takes a **LOT OF PLUCK!**

150

What's a **GHOST'S** favourite Christmas **ENTERTAINMENT?**

**A PHANTOMIME!**

**Did you KNOW?**

Pantomimes have been popular shows for over 200 years!

151

KNOCK KNOCK.
Who's there?
HOWARD. Howard who?
HOWARD YOU LIKE to sing CHRISTMAS CAROLS with me?

152

What did MRS. CLAUS say to SANTA CLAUS when she looked up in the SKY?

"LOOKS LIKE RAIN, DEAR."

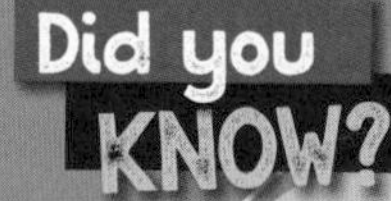


Candy canes were invented to keep children quiet in church!

153

What did ADAM say the day before CHRISTMAS?

"IT'S CHRISTMAS, EVE!"

154

My niece put something SUSPICIOUS in my car this winter. . . I think it was AUNTIE-FREEZE!

155

Why did the REINDEER get MARRIED?

It was LOVE AT FROST SIGHT!

156

Where does BOXING DAY come before Christmas?

In the DICTIONARY!

157

KNOCK KNOCK. Who's there? YAH. Yah who? OH MY, someone's really EXCITED about Christmas!

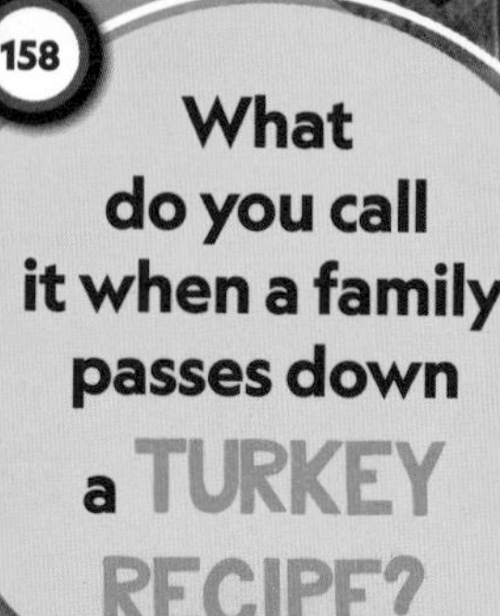

158

What do you call it when a family passes down a TURKEY RECIPE?

COPY AND BASTING!

159

Did you hear about the family that went on a CHRISTMAS DAY SKI TRIP? It started off fine, but went downhill fast.

Did you KNOW?

The Nordmann fir is the most popular type of Christmas tree in Europe.

LOL!

160 The snowman's toddler was having a TEMPER TANTRUM... it was a real meltdown!

161 How do you wish a DOG MERRY CHRISTMAS?

FELIZ NAVI-DOG!

162 What did the KIDS' MOTHER say after they finished opening PRESENTS?

OH, WHAT A CHRISTMESS!

HA HA HA

163 KNOCK KNOCK. Who's there? NORMA LEE. Norma Lee who? NORMA LEE we have TURKEY at Christmas.

164 How does CHRISTMAS DAY END?

With a Y

165 What do you get if you cross a turkey and a CENTIPEDE?

Drumsticks for everyone at CHRISTMAS!

Did you KNOW?

Traditionally decorations stay up until the 12th Night of Christmas – or 5 January!

# FAMILY FUN

166 Sister:
What are you giving MUM and DAD for Christmas?
Brother:
A list of everything I want!

167 Daughter:
Can I have a PONY for Christmas?
Dad: The oven's only big enough for a TURKEY!

168 You can catch me but not throw me.
I'm very popular in DECEMBER.
What am I?

A COLD!

169

**KNOCK KNOCK.** Who's there? **FREEZE.** Freeze who? **FREEZE** a jolly good fellow!

LOL!

170

What kind of **BALL** doesn't **BOUNCE?**

A SNOWBALL

171

How does a **PENGUIN** build a **TOY HOUSE?**

IGLOOS it together!

# IT'S SNOW JOKE!

72

One evening a VIKING named RUDOLPH the RED was looking out of the window when he said, "We're in for a STORMY NIGHT." His wife asked, "How can you tell?" "Because RUDOLPH THE RED KNOWS RAIN, DEAR."

**Did you KNOW?**

There were only 7 white Christmases in the UK in the whole 20th century!

173

Why was the LITTLE GIRL SO COLD on Christmas morning?

Because it was DECEMBRRRRRR!

174

Which is faster, HOT or COLD?

HOT, because it's much easier to catch COLD!

175

**KNOCK KNOCK.** Who's there? Icy. Icy who? **ICY YOU!**

## Did you KNOW?

60 million Christmas trees are grown every year in Europe.

176

What did the **ICY ROAD** say to the car?

Want to go for A SPIN?

177

Which **WINTER SPORT** do trees enjoy?

AL-PINE SKIING

# IT'S SNOW JOKE!

178

Who is a SNOWMAN'S favourite RAPPER?

ICE CUBE

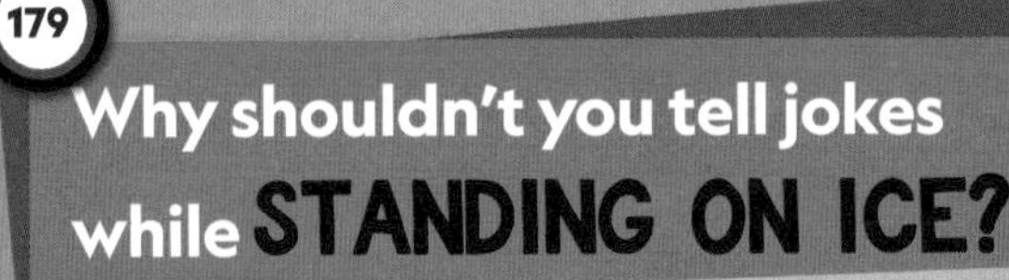

179

Why shouldn't you tell jokes while STANDING ON ICE?

You don't want it to CRACK UP!

180

When is a BOAT just like SNOW?

When it's ADRIFT!

Why was the SNOWMAN embarrassed when he was spotted rummaging through a BAG OF CARROTS?

He was caught PICKING HIS NOSE!

What do SNOWMEN EAT for lunch?

ICEBERGERS!

How does a SNOWMAN get around?

On an ICICLE

# FREEZY DOES IT!

184

Why does everyone LOVE FROSTY the SNOWMAN?

He's COOL!

185

What did one SNOWMAN say to the other?

Do you smell CARROTS?

**Did you KNOW?**

The world's biggest snowman stood 34 m tall.

186

What do you get when you cross a SNOWMAN and a VAMPIRE?

FROSTBITE

187

What did FROSTY'S GIRLFRIEND do when she was angry at him?

Gave him the COLD SHOULDER!

188

What do you call an OLD snowman?

WATER

OH-OH

189

What do snowmen wear on their HEADS?

Ice CAPS!

# FREEZY DOES IT!

What's a snowman's favourite SCHOOL ACTIVITY?

SNOW AND TELL

**Did you KNOW?**

Every snowflake has a unique pattern – but they all have six sides.

What should you say to a STRESSED-OUT snowman?

CHILL OUT!

How do snowmen say GOODBYE?

HAVE AN ICE DAY!

KNOCK KNOCK.
Who's there?
AVERY. Avery who?
AVERY MERRY CHRISTMAS to you!

What did the POLICEMAN say when he saw a SNOWMAN STEALING?

FREEZE!

What do SNOWMEN call their offspring?

CHILL-DREN

# FREEZY DOES IT!

**Did you KNOW?** The earliest illustration of a snowman is in a book written in 1380!

196

What kind of ANDROIDS do you find in the ARCTIC?

SNOW-BOTS

197

Why shouldn't you TRUST snowmen?

They're always up to SNOW GOOD!

198

Why did the snowman name his PET DOG Frost?

Because FROST BITES!

199

**KNOCK KNOCK.** Who's there? **OLIVE.** Olive who? **OLIVE THE OTHER REINDEER** used to laugh and call him names...

200

What do you call a **BLIND REINDEER?**

NO-EYE DEER

201

What do **REINDEER** say before they tell a joke?

"This one will **SLEIGH YOU!**"

# FURRY FUNNIES

202

How do **SHEEP** wish each other happy holidays?

MERRY CHRISTMAS TO EWE!

203

What's green, covered in baubles and goes **"RIBBIT, RIBBIT"?**

A MISTLE-TOAD!

**Did you KNOW?**

Santa has 9 magical reindeer: Dasher, Dancer, Prancer, Vixen, Comet, Cupid, Donner, Blitzen and Rudolph.

204

Who delivers presents to baby **SHARKS?**

SANTA JAWS

## Did you KNOW?

Reindeer are also known as caribou.

205 **KNOCK KNOCK.** Who's there? **RUDE-OLPH.** Rude-olph wh-? **DO YOU MIND** if I **INTERRUPT?!**

206 Which of **SANTA'S REINDEER** loved to party?

DANCER

207 Why didn't **RUDOLPH** go to **SCHOOL?**

He was ELF-TAUGHT!

208 What do you call a reindeer with **THREE EYES?**

A REIIINDEER

209 What do you call a **BLIND REINDEER** with **NO LEGS?**

Still NO-EYE DEER

210

**Which one of Santa's reindeer can you see in OUTER SPACE?**

COMET

211

## Who did Rudolph invite to his CHRISTMAS PARTY?

His DEER-EST FRIENDS!

212

## What do you call a YETI with a six-pack?

The ABDOMINAL SNOWMAN!

213

## When do COWS open their presents?

OXING DAY!

# FURRY FUNNIES

## Did you KNOW?

Male reindeer can grow up to 1.2 m tall at the shoulder and weigh up to 250 kg.

**214** Why don't LOBSTERS give Christmas presents?

They're SHELLFISH

**215** How long should a REINDEER'S LEGS be?

Long enough TO REACH THE GROUND

**216** How does RUDOLPH know when Christmas is coming?

He checks his CALEN-DEER!

217

What do you call a **CAT** on the **BEACH** on Christmas Day?

SANDY CLAWS.

**Did you KNOW?**

Reindeer spend 40% of their lives in snow and have hollow fur to trap heat.

218

How did **RUDOLPH** survive his first trip with **SANTA?**

He held on for DEER LIFE!

219

Which of Santa's reindeer are **DINOSAURS** afraid of?

COMET

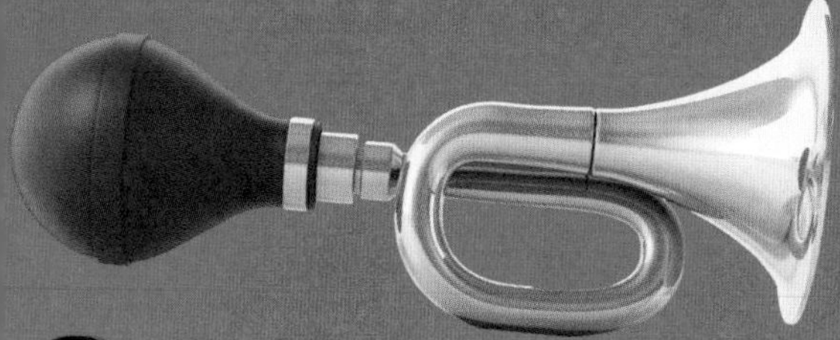

220 Why do reindeer WEAR BELLS?

Their horns DON'T WORK!

221 Why do BIRDS FLY SOUTH for Christmas?

It's too far TO WALK!

222 Where do CATS KISS at Christmas?

Under the MIAOW-STLETOE!

223

## Why don't reindeer like **PICNICS?**

Because of all their ANT-LURES!

224

## What's a **DOG'S** favourite Christmas **CAROL?**

BARK, THE HERALD ANGELS SING

225

## How does a **SHEEP** say "Happy Christmas"?

FLEECE NAVIDAD!

# FURRY FUNNIES

226 Why didn't Rudolph get a good REPORT CARD?

Because he went down in HISTORY!

227 What did the GRUMPY SHEEP say when his friends wished him Merry Christmas?

BAAAA HUMBUG!

228 Why did no one bid for Donner and Blitzen on EBAY?

Because they were TWO DEER!

**Did you KNOW?**

Reindeer are good swimmers!

229 What do DUCKS go to the THEATRE for at Christmas?

To watch the NUT-QUACKER!

Quack Quack!

230 What GAME do reindeer play at PARTIES?

TRUTH-OR-DEER

231 Why can't you SHOCK reindeer?

They've HERD IT ALL!

232 Who leads Santa's SLEIGH UNDERWATER?

RU-DOLPHIN!

# FURRY FUNNIES

233 Who won the **RACE** between Rudolph and Prancer?

Rudolph won by a NOSE!

234 What do you give an **ARTISTIC DOG** for Christmas?

A FETCH-A-SKETCH!

## Did you KNOW?

The Sámi people of northern Norway, Sweden and Finland really do use reindeer to pull sleighs through the snow.

235
## How do **DOGS** know when Santa has arrived?

They can hear hooves tapping **ON THE WOOF!**

236
## Why do **CATS** take so long to wrap Christmas presents?

They want them to be **PURR-FECT!**

237
## What's a cat's favourite **TOPPING** for Christmas **PUDDING?**

**MICE CREAM!**

### Did you KNOW?

**The name Santa Claus comes from Sinterklaas, which means Saint Nicholas in Dutch!**

238 **Why didn't the CAT like the toy he got for Christmas?**

It wasn't up to SCRATCH!

239 **How do SNAKES solve their Christmas Day arguments?**

They HISS AND MAKE UP!

240 **Where do you find REINDEER?**

I dunno, depends on WHERE YOU LEFT THEM!

241 KNOCK KNOCK. Who's there? DEXTER. Dexter who? DEXTER HALLS with boughs of HOLLY...

**Did you KNOW?**

Movie-makers once used untoasted cornflakes as "snow"!

242 How does Darth Vader prefer his Christmas TURKEY MEAT?

ON THE DARK SIDE!

243 How did SCROOGE score a goal in the football match?

THE GHOST OF CHRISTMAS PASSED!

# MOVIE MIRTH

244 I got a universal REMOTE CONTROL for Christmas. This changes everything.

245 Why wouldn't Scrooge eat at the PASTA restaurant?

IT COST A PRETTY PENNE!

246 In what way are Christmas trees like BLOCKBUSTER MOVIES?

THEY BOTH HAVE STARS!

247 KNOCK KNOCK. Who's there? ALLIE. Allie who? ALLIE WANT FOR CHRISTMAS IS YOU.

248 What do you call a Christmas romcom about BREAD?

LOAF ACTUALLY

249 What did Luke Skywalker say after he PLANTED a Christmas tree farm?

MAY THE FOREST BE WITH YOU!

## Did you KNOW?

The much-loved Christmas film "It's a Wonderful Life" was a flop when it first came out!

# MOVIE MIRTH

250 Why does The Grinch enjoy **GARDENING?**

HE'S GOT A GREEN FINGERS

251 What does Elsa put in Olaf's **STOCKING** for Christmas?

A LUMP OF COLD!

252 What's a bird's favourite **CHRISTMAS FILM?**

"THE FINCH WHO STOLE CHRISTMAS"

253

KNOCK KNOCK. Who's there? DEWEY. Dewey who? DEWEY KNOW how long it is until Santa gets here?

254

Why couldn't the SKELETON go to the Christmas party?

Because he had NO BODY TO GO WITH!

## Did you KNOW?

The biggest ever Secret Santa included 30,000 people!

255

What do you call a SNOWMAN PARTY?

A SNOWBALL

# HAVING A BALL

256

What kind of Christmas carol do you sing to **FRUIT?**

We Wish You A BERRY CHRISTMAS

257

What did one **ANGEL** say to the other?

HALO THERE!

LOL!

258

How do **DONKEYS** say hello at the Christmas party?

MULE-TIDE GREETINGS!

259

**KNOCK KNOCK.** Who's there?
**HONDA.** Honda who?
**HONDA FIRST DAY OF CHRISTMAS** my true love sent to me...

260

What did the **STAMP** say to the **CHRISTMAS CARD?**

Stick with me and **WE'LL GO PLACES!**

261

Which **FOOTBALL** team puts on the best nativity play?

**MANGER-STER UNITED!**

## Did you KNOW?

The tallest Christmas tree stood 67.4 m – higher than Nelson's Column! The Douglas fir tree was decorated in Seattle, USA in 1950.

# HAPPY DAYS ARE HERE AGAIN!

262

What do ANGRY MICE send to each other at Christmas?

CROSS-MOUSE CARDS!

263

What part of the BODY do you only see during Christmas?

The MISTLE-TOE!

264

Why was the last GINGERBREAD MAN left on the plate sad?

He wasn't good at BAKING NEW FRIENDS!

265 **KNOCK KNOCK.** Who's there? **LUKE.** Luke who? **LUKE AT ALL** those presents!

266 What do you call buying a **PIANO** for the holidays?

CHRISTMAS CHOPIN!

267 Why are **CHRISTMAS TREES** so fond of the past?

Because the present's BENEATH THEM!

**Did you KNOW?**

6 million rolls of sticky tape are sold before Christmas in the UK!

268 Last Christmas I bought my friend a **LIE DETECTOR** as a gift. "Oh... I love it!" she said. "We'll see," I said.

# THE GIFT OF LAUGHTER

269 I bought my son a **FRIDGE** for Christmas. I can't wait to see his face **LIGHT UP** when he opens it.

270 How do elves show their **WORK** off in school?

They PRESENT IT!

271

## Why was E the ONLY LETTER that got a Christmas present?

Because all the other letters were "NOT-E"!

272

## What's a child's FAVOURITE KING at Christmas?

A STOC-KING!

273

## Why are MUMMIES such big fans of Christmas?

Because they enjoy WRAPPING!

### Did you KNOW?

A survey showed that more people buy Christmas presents for their pets than for their friends!

# THE GIFT OF LAUGHTER

274 I have this incredible ability to predict what's inside a **WRAPPED PRESENT**. It's a gift.

275 The only Christmas present that I got this year was a deck of **STICKY PLAYING CARDS**. I find that very hard to deal with.

276 What's the best **CHRISTMAS PRESENT** you can get?

A broken drum - YOU CAN'T BEAT IT!

277

KNOCK KNOCK.
Who's there?
GLADYS. Gladys who? GLADYS FINALLY CHRISTMAS!

278

What do you call a REINDEER GHOST?

CARI-BOO!

Did you KNOW?

There are 364 gifts in total in the "12 Days of Christmas" song!

279

Did you hear about the CHEESY comedian?

He had some CRACKERS!

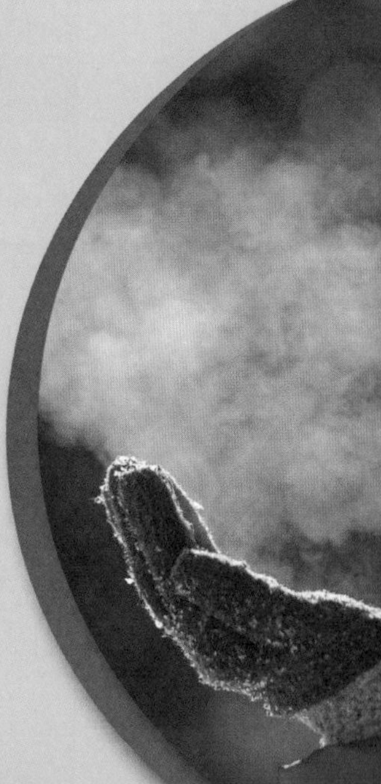

# IT'S THE MOST PUN-DERFUL TIME OF THE YEAR!

What did the **THIRD WISE MAN** say after his friends had already presented **GOLD** and frankincense?

But wait – THERE'S MYRRH!

How do elves get to the **TOP FLOOR?**

In the ELF-EVATOR!

You can only see me when it's **COLD OUTSIDE.** What am I?

Your BREATH

**KNOCK KNOCK.** Who's there? **HOLLY.** Holly who? **HOLLY-DAYS** are here again.

What do you call an **ART MUSEUM** made out of ice?

The IG-LOUVRE!

285

Why don't **PENGUINS** fly?

They're not tall enough to be PILOTS!

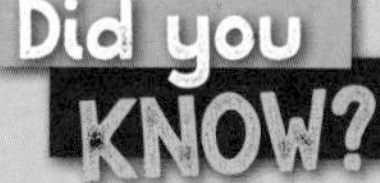


300 million mince pies are eaten every Christmas.

# IT'S THE MOST PUN-DERFUL TIME OF THE YEAR!

**286**

What did the **BEAVER** say to the Christmas tree?

NICE GNAWING YOU!

**287**

What makes Christmas the most competitive **HOLIDAY?**

It's in the WIN-TER!

**288**

Why shouldn't you live in an **ADVENT CALENDAR?**

IT'S GOT 24 DOORS AND NO WINDOWS!

**KNOCK KNOCK.** Who's there? **YULE.** Yule who? **YULE BE SORRY** if you don't open this door!

What's **WHITE** and goes up?

A confused SNOWFLAKE

Did you hear about the man who stole an **ADVENT CALENDAR?** He got 25 days!

BANG!

**Did you KNOW?**

The biggest Christmas cracker ever made was 45 m long!

# IT'S THE MOST PUN-DERFUL TIME OF THE YEAR!

**292**

Where can you find a **CHRISTMAS TREE?**

In between CHRISTMAS TWO and CHRISTMAS FOUR!

**293**

Did you hear about the **CAT** that tried to **DECORATE** the Christmas tree?

It was a CAT-ASTROPHE!

**294**

Why does the Christmas **ALPHABET** only have 25 letters?

There's NO L!

295

**KNOCK KNOCK.**
Who's there?
**NOAH.** Noah who?
**NOAH GOOD CHRISTMAS JOKE?**

296

What do you call a Christmas tree that finds **ALGEBRA TRICKY?**

STUMPED!

297

Did you hear about the child who refused to tie his **SHOES** properly?

He ended up on the KNOTTY LIST!

Did you KNOW?

The average Christmas tree is 15 years old when it is used.

# IT'S THE MOST PUN-DERFUL TIME OF THE YEAR!

**298**

The Christmas **JUMPER** my kids gave me last year kept picking up static electricity. I took it back and exchanged it for another one – free of charge.

**299**

How did Mary and Joseph tell how **HEAVY** Jesus was?

They had a WEIGH IN THE MANGER!

**300**

What does the month of **DECEMBER** have that no other month does?

The letter "D".

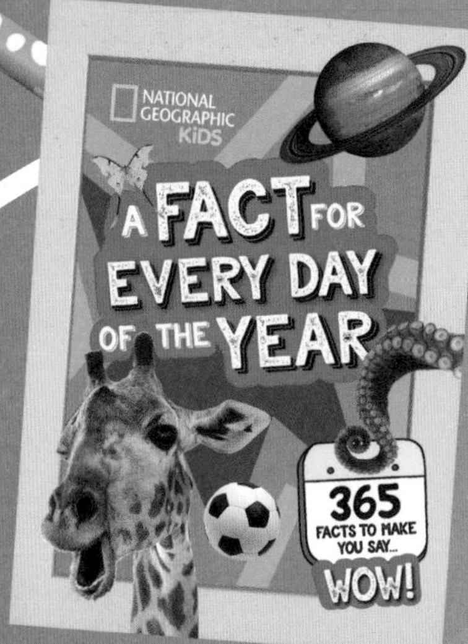


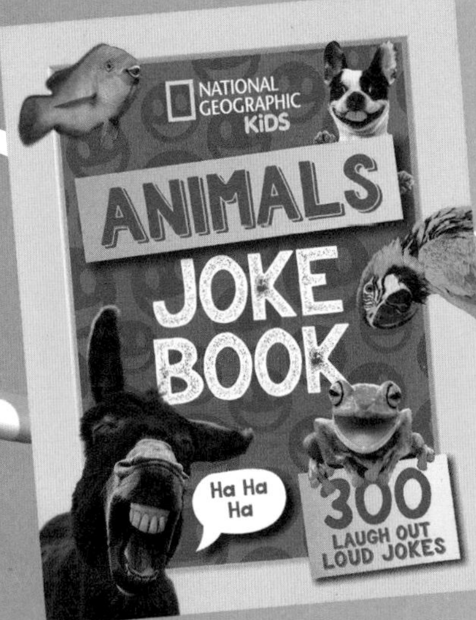


NATIONAL GEOGRAPHIC KiDS